Gathering the
Waters

Gathering the Waters
by Keisha-Gaye Anderson

Gathering the Waters

Copyright © 2014 Keisha-Gaye Anderson
ISBN 978-0-9912975-2-8
Published by Jamii Publishing
San Bernardino, CA
www.JamiiPublishing.com

Cover art by Angelina Blasich
Cover design by Jamii Publishing 2014

Acknowledgements:

I would like to thank the following publications for publishing poems in this collection: Streetnotes: Cross Cultural Poetics, Afrobeat Journal, Black Renaissance Noire, Small Axe Salon, Caribbean in Transit Arts Journal, Killens Review of Arts and Letters, Promethean: The Literary Journal of The City University of New York, For the Crowns of Your Heads, Poetry in Performance, Women Writers in Bloom, African Voices Magazine, The Mom Egg, Anthology of the Americas Poetry Festival of New York, and Mosaic Literary Magazine.

Most of all, I would like to thank my husband and my children for their loving support and inspiration, which has sustained me on this journey, and helped me to remember that all things are possible.

For the Ancestors.

Gathering
the Waters

Table of Contents

the Dream Time

the Dream Time
gathers me
pulls me back
to painted sky
forgotten colors
warm earth
of our
before/thoughts
where real mirrors
refract my whirling
soul into the
darkness

just for a moment

the Dream Time
escape hatch
reality check
floodgates
where droplets
bounce back
to sea
swirl free
in shapeless
        knowing

formless
                    loving
every thing
that is
                              We

the Dream Time
remembrance
and reminders
of the why
of I,
colossus builder
tracker of errant
notes
lover
        always
woman
                this   time
dancer afloat
cosmos
lovely chaos
cloaked in black light
penetrates
cracks
of this false order
clocks
commerce
slaughter

4

the Dream Time
all time
no time
every time
the one thread
is the whole
tapestry
all the majesty
and misery
these forms
come to be
when we spy
ourselves
through the
peephole
of creation
a spiraling sphere
of sensations

the Dreamer
sees all
at once
draws her bow
mends the
fissures
with golden
chords

heart spun
notes
that hum low
trickle
into botanicas
kumina drums
smoke of sage
and sunday hymns

the human
feels only
the walls
around him

Have You Seen my Mother?

Have you seen my mother?

Her face is a cool midnight
skin perfumed like a summer rain

I fell from her belly at 3 a.m.
through the keyhole
of a question
about pain

And I descended,
a dazzling light,
diving downward
into voices
and days

First, I was molten
then stone
then, forgot my name,
my home

Tell me,
do you know my ma?

Her voice rumbles like

a sweet thunder
hums like waves breaking
on a coral shore

Her hair twists like a bramble
firm and free
and all that's left of her tongue
is a rhythm in me

Do you know where she is?
Does she love me?
Can she see these brick
pillows I have learned not to
feel?

Will she whisper
through my tears that
this is not real?

Stones

We tumbled into this life
knowing how to become stones
us star light gate keepers
who pushed the world
through our wombs
in the onyx dawn of
chaos

Only to stumble in the
night
over discarded petticoats
suckle babies not our own
warm the bodies of creatures
thinking themselves men
fan flies away from fish
for a tuppence worth of
hope
muzzle identity
and culture's melody
to clean toilets
in the land of plenty
squeeze curves into
less magnificent molds
to keep the sun out of their
eyes

and bend smiles
into white flags
to dodge hatchets
in the corporate gauntlet

Yes,
Mamma knows
how to become like granite
take the licks
become inert
in order to remain
just remain
on this earth

But don't judge me for being rough
my children
because inside this tamarind heart
is a churning volcano
ready to erupt for you
rain black earth
onto concrete
so you can take root
and grow yourself
into a new rainbow

See through all of
our eyes
and recognize

the constellation
of your existence
formed from the primordial dust
of those who resisted

Shape thoughts
that forge a new world
from our burning hearts
destroy the illusion
custom fit for our vision
imitations of life
clawing at the risen

Stand on the foundation
of my soul, my children,
and make me molten
once more
so I can explode into new worlds
paint colors your eyes can't see

> *Set the captives free*
> *Set the captives free*

It's time for an avalanche of love
to put ignorance out of its
misery
reveal the mystery
in the seed of life

that flows through every
artery

Open our beings
to the buried memory
that rides on a shooting star
drop the masquerade
of identity
become fully
what we are

From Ile-Ife

They took my mother's body
from Ile-Ife
back then
during that time
when she adorned herself with gold dust
and birthed men of bronze
between her thoughts and her fingertips
and could raise any tide into a tempest
with a mere flourish of her skirt

They hammered her into an industry
a copy machine
to fund a journey
that should have been navigated
in their own thoughts,
and gorged on a bounty that could never
bring them immortality
or make them see their own reflections

They built this city
and other sprawling cogs
in those used-to-be places
greased by our sweat
just to manufacture fear

But I am still here
in my mother's skin
swaying through these streets
to the rhythm
of my beating heart
a hymn to the one true reality
and carry always with me
the majesty and mystery
that is the Great Mother

Maps

They want to hear
my story of "foreign"
these sun-loved faces
standing arms akimbo
in the bosom of blue mountains
where abengs still sound in ceremony
'longside djembe drums
and pregnant silence

Bougainvilleas
poincianas
roasting things
arrest my senses
sing with the greatest part of me
unnamable and beyond skin

I blink slowly
breathe deep
tell them that we are the story
righting ourselves
leaving music every place we enter
serenading strangers to the song of
living

But there are still questions in their eyes

as they peak into the cupboards of my mind

I try to tell them that
whatever is useful in there
looks like a travelers palm
misty waterfall
bashful mimosa

But I know
they will have to make their own maps
see for themselves

Whose Story

She eyes my locks
wrinkles her nose
asks if I'm
going to keep my hair like that
forever

How can I fathom forever
I say
when I don't even know
yesterday?

Dropped into the middle
of this book
I make my own
way

Take pleasure
in the undulating
form of this self
and let it
be
simply because
I can

Summer of Silence

I didn't mean to tell her about the rape
that summer of silence between us

We should have been like friends by then, like the
books said

Me and my mother
22 and 50
cut from the same burlap of St. Ann

"You ah nuh big woman"
she said, seasoning that ever-bubbling pot
with everything else unspoken

My ears were harder then
thoughts scaling another wall of a man
addicted to the elixir of my hips

Our wild dances drummed away the silence
for a time

Then spring

"I'm sorry about 1997," she wrote
on a Post-it, slapped on sideways

inside my
birthday card

I wondered
how many of her own memories
she'd pasted over, put away

What substance of silence
lay beyond the dam of those eyes
whose tears had dried up

I decided
she knew exactly how I'd left my body
under the weight of his encroaching flesh

That she had good reason to tell me half a story,
out of the blue,
about a boy with an ice pick
prying through her zinc roof
when she was a girl

I understand to
let the steam swell the rice
don't stir the pot
stand next to her
in the quiet
and wait for our dams
to break

wash us free of
memory

Memory

She thought she was a Lady
on all those caffeine mornings
of sucking in and pressing out
and force-fitting overlaid ideals
onto youthful expectations

but she was only female
in the front of her mind,
at least,

born of a long line of females
stripped of the right to adornment
and male admiration
without conflagration in the pews
and the stigma of being an elixir
strong enough to wake the cadavers

It's your fault they take you...

you are too much yourselves
honey hips, the shape of life
telling lips that could expose the whole
irony
of this thing they call reality
and hum the puzzle pieces into place
for all to see
turn the game on its head

make them cease to be
those canopies painted like heaven
held up by her hands
blocking out the true light—
punishment for being what they were not

She is swimming
in a fantasy of femininity
a backward vision
surrounded by dead ends

but lies only borrow breath
because memory is the ocean of the
infinite
that swallows convention
and is older than even her
reflection
so when full recognition
comes back
there is only that

Just the truth

and sound of laughter
because she will know then
that she was always

Woman

Fire Woman

What a way she bright, though,
eeh?
dat fat gyal
dat fiyah woman

Is who she think she is?

Market hips
rocking like
a rum shop
before day light
rolling like a river
swelling to meet sea
after the devil and
him wife did ah fight
flashing tears
from the clouds
streaking the faces
of hibiscus
pulling colors through the curtain
of the sky

See her there,
rainbow snake charmer
higgler

rude girl
Mami Wata woman
wind chime laughter
shattering
the queen's english
morning stride
twisting greenwich mean time

A carnival of adornment
from the temple of her
ankles
to the crown of her head

Red hair
green hair
no hair—
she nuh business
and black, she black, she black
so till

Till she become a memory
and a promise
a double dare
a heckle in the
sunday mass
a line in the sand
cross it,
if yu tink yuh bad

A body tolerating
uniforms of commerce
all for the sake of a tightly packed barrel
school fees
and lay away on satin and sequins
designed to hug every living curve

Don't command her
don't test
or expect
the original holy word
to be unsheathed
from the holster of her mouth
and linger
near your ear
until just the right time
until you get comfortable
forget to use
the code words
the safe slurs

Third world
Urban
Inner city
Under privileged
Disadvantaged
Developing

Primitive

All flimsy arrows aimed
at pernicious life
sailing through
stardust template
pre-time goddess
unscathed

She is still here
from clarendon to brooklyn
call her Iris, Lilith
call her Isis, Kali
call her savvy

But don't call her out
her name

She's got no use
for girdles and bleaching cream
coconut milk never killed
anybody
candles and white rum have their place
everything inna darkness
must
come
to
light

She's got stamina for the
marathon of creation
sucks her teeth
at your corsets
for jubilation
blinders wrapped
in greenbacks
promises called
pensions

And she will wait
as long as it
takes for her garden to
grow
for her children to
know

OCD II

It starts with the fixing of things,
adjusting, tweaking
position ever-so-perfect
that one try won't do
and you find yourself
locked
in motion
endless repetition
torturous desire for
perfection
which has eluded
every other layer of your
being

So there is now
only the object
sitting cruelly in front of you
hopelessly imperfect
needing your expert touch
but you too are flawed
to affect much

You are
the sum of a cycle
of lives equally flawed

and wearily traveled

Who will you be
what will it teach you,
when you know for certain
who you really are?

Sisters

she spun herself
into a grey
cocoon
and arrived
at my front door

between jobs
and beyond inspiration
again

mental illness,
she says

bullshit,
I say

but,
she is my sister

wears our mother's
face
and is just as
plucky
when the spirit
moves her

I let her stay
twist my ear
in circles
and then
dismiss me
with acid tongue
and side glance of
guilt

her mind is a
wild bull
a shriek
in the gut of a
slave ship

perhaps,
this is her last
memory
before waking up here
perhaps,
I was there too

she cooks
I light a blue candle
which she calls
folly

I call on the mothers
I do not know
ask if they are
looking for us
ask if they know
we are still lost

I Am the Caribbean

In the belly of a ship named
for supposed nobility
I came this way

From low-caste Bombay
to Chinese-built railway
I came this way

From Irish town here
poor as the one back there
I came this way

I became that jigsaw piece
floating on the archipelago
too enmeshed to go
beyond the gravity of
my being

I am the Caribbean

a sweltering pool
of disjointed life
every day remaking
reshaping itself
into an electric rhythm

skipping from
batá
to tassa
to nyabinghi
weaving through me

Making me

that kumina sound
that pan melody
that flute in the hills
that shak shak
that brings back
that sound of conviction
of personhood fought for
the independent ardor
that we bled to see

I came to be

that diasporic medley
calling me down
to ride through this life
changing shape as I see fit
and though we may forget
the names of spirit
we call them viscerally

to Trench Town
Port-au-Prince
Port of Spain
concrete just the same
all repositories
of potential energy
and stilted memory

I am the Caribbean

Enough

Razor cane cutting skin
in fields that whisper the old names
was enough

Dirty drawers left there like a mockery
of backs too tired, too young
was enough

All the double-edged smiles
shielding daggers
destined for those who
Possessed the Secret of Joy
is enough.

We've been on a mission
kicking stones
for signs of life
but they only hurl themselves
and their misgivings
at the living to draw blood
in search of answers to that question
wedged in their minds:

What is God?

So, no more gluing together
mosaics with cracked glass
for future perfect worlds
they only diffuse the light
distort the picture

It ends now.

The Earth is tired
of sending symphonies
through the breasts of birds
that will be only felled by hunters
for sport
and left to rot
near hungry belly children

She is tired of swallowing her beautiful
incarnations too soon
because boredom is remedied
by squeezing the trigger
at whatever dares
to become a man

Enough wailing mothers
and pundits lull-a-buying
sleep walkers

Let the Earth quake

and absorb its anomalies
who only see through
the prism of the dollar

Let the waters swell and
sink the machines
that dig our graves

Let the tempests inhale and
throw their bosoms
onto glass fortresses
skirted by weary men
with only
the skin on their backs
and sewer grates for blankets

The floodlights of a new dawn
must incinerate the cobwebs
of consciousness
so that the Real
can shed its shapes
and be eternally itself

So that new colors
can come once again
into view
for those who have been forced
to hide their sight

So that the wheel can
lets us off
we can finally leave
this carnival

It's time for time
to end and for
Life to begin

There has been enough of
droplets falling from the one big sky
and bouncing into
civil wars

There is more to this
than a full stomach
and stock options
There is a splendor waiting
to explode from inside
each willing body

There has been enough suffering
and too many forgotten questions

This is the final chance
to find the road map home

Will we step off
the precipice
into eternity
or keep treading in the
big sea?

Stages

When my daughter came
my back went
collapsing like a controlled
explosion

The doctor said
it was only a matter of time
that the problem was my height

There I was
sliced into two
22 staples
over an ugly gash
over-spent sick days
new mortgage running late
dirty laundry
bad drugs
that drew cold sweat
and expletives

That's when I called her
sister/friend
with sandy brown arms
course hands
and courser wit

She rode the train
from Rockaway
carrying her hood dryer
and shampoo
like a medicine bag
parted my hair
into diamonds
greased my scalp
twisted these tresses into a
tapestry
to remind me of
who I have always been

Barer of the covenant
before the bible
link in the lattice work of reality
cradler of visions
and maker of ways

Present

I know,
have always known
this voice

Brass bells swinging on a
blue morning
breath/hymn to
creation
music of the spheres
and song of this body,
that asks and gives
and moves like a lantern
across today

Forward is
the motion
natural and inevitable
when sight is clear

But I am here
running in place
butting up against a lie
that I do not
fit this puzzle
weave this circle

you call culture

I remember
how it all fell
when the names
were burned
and we were given
amnesia

I know the gold
currency of my skin
cannot forget the ocean
of Mami's tears

My children are tired of
falling into flesh
swinging machetes
making ways
for your passage

I will not disappear
to quell shockwaves
of eyes shut
in unison

Words come like piss
urgent and noisy
and everywhere

there are mirrors

In the dark
you will thank me for finding you
with the torch
of my song

Where We Are

"Babylon, you can't study the Rastaman."
                    —Joseph 'Culture' Hill

How did we get
here,
people?
Where our story
has slipped into parody
become a mystery
an echo in the
dark
a faint memory
pushing phobias
into the
today-psyche?

Children of the sun,
how has your
chiseled legacy
become merely
an anomaly
cracking this surface
life,
an anathema
to profit,

a template for
mass produced culture,
acid burning holes in
safe nostalgia?

No wonder you're angry.

Mask

Do not remove your mask
here,
my sister

not yet

there is too much unraveling
left to do
so many becomings
hinging on your memory
of you

and every oil rig
and chemical
disguised as food
every anti-psychotic
fed to babies
every sterilized womb
every somebody grateful
they weren't born as black
and brown
as you

every single one of them
is a blessed lightening bolt

waking your heart
to its black whole
pulling together
your shattered pieces
to reassemble
the monolith that is
you
blasted to pieces
the ALL
became two

For them that cut cane
tie bows around dukunoo
pull sweet grass into baskets
give lyrics to the blues
sing cantos dos orixás
make balms out of house plants
turn tears into flamenco
and put the sway in belly dance

I say to you:

Stand your ground
adorn your countenance
become a legend
but meet the people
where they are

because this dream is
a west-bound train
heading for a cliff
a race from panic
calling itself progress
so be the honey music that
bends the tracks
alters the route

And bury the earth's heart beat
in the back room of their minds
lure them to the dance
of their existence
through the
bacchanal
of your
smile

Don't
think

Simply
be

Don't look for the answer
in any four walls
prove there are no walls

And lay out your best
peacock feathers
cowry shells
white lace
and over proof rum
for the journey
the path
el camino
this trip
that you chip chip chip
down the roads
of creation
to the percussion
of your hips

Grow away from the
circles of madness
but keep your wings
concealed
lest the people startle
and kill the
premonition
that is you
a template for
the real

Your kindness

must be well aimed
pedestrian
conjured through hugs
and verse
squeezed through fingers
unafraid of dirt

Your words must
ride with the trends
float parallel to party music
and fill the spaces of silence
that punctuate
the noise of living

So, wear this body out, girl
let it earn its breath
die awake,
if you dare
if you're lucky
if you can see

Re-create our forgotten home
from the blueprint
of your secret name

We're waiting on you
to change the game

River Mama

The baba is familiar
like how my grandmother
sucks her teeth
always before a chuckle

Candle-lit room
concrete/wood kaleidoscope
electric with
invisible chatter
threatens to
pull me out
through my head
dance me free me of
this upside down reality

But I summon a will
faintly remembered
and know exactly how to
stand still
listen to his words
already revealed in my
5 a.m. dream

I am draped in white
trying to run

always running

A hand
holds me still
that same hand
throwing these bones
telling me
the Lady of the Water is
calling me

I know this
the message is the same
each year
with each messenger

Why won't I dive in
lead this family
out of the loop
of suffering
spawned across the Atlantic?

We are drowning in
this illusion
spun by those
dressing up in Christ
who still count us
like inventory
peddle poison to cure cancer

validate gratitude
for daughters with fare skin
tell us to pop a pill
for every passing trouble

Don't worry, mother
I have not forgotten you
I am just wading in
just wading in

Survival

If I were to tune my ears
to the narrow sliver
of noise
called modern life
I would hear only
a farewell chant
a requiem
a choir yelling:

The world no longer needs
you
don't want your kind
'round here
no more

But reality speaks louder
cherry blossoms curtsey
when they see me coming
clouds saunter over head
sawyin hips big like mine
birds and butterflies
are the sum of the same
math that made this body
made my hair stand up like
an army

warms my center
into a welcome place for
ether to gather
and make life
and make life
and make life

You
can
never
erase
me

The Academy

The academy wants artifice
eloquent erasure
spreadsheets in the black
new donors with old names
a stream of carbon copy bodies
that lift
scrub
lay down
push paper
with a smile
and never ask
how we even
got here
why food is chemistry
why poverty runs in the
family

What I have to say
won't be filed in ivy walls
places with protocols
against spontaneous joy

This heart/speech
is saying
has said

bares repeating
still

These words roll
bounce between the lips
of the sisters who bend my locks into
sculpture

These ideas
drip down the backs of
unnamed builders, concrete churners
who work always
off the books

This speech floats through the asylum
and in between lion cages
called solitary confinement

This me today
sees you
cannot not see you
knows that you are
dancing on my neck

I must speak
always speak
with the inherited breath
that carries me through this drudgery

for a little fresh food
and a 2 a.m. space to dream
unexplored ideas
damned good poetry
that evaporates under heavy lids
piles of bills
asking eyes of children
throbbing feet
following alone-ness
in crowded rooms
of suits and practiced laughter

All structures
will fall

Amnesia

I have never had full amnesia
so every mirror
confirms
a comely mask
but begs a more pressing question:

What is your mission?
This time?

Because a solder's stride
has always propelled my thoughts
led my eyes
to the disquieted ether
to the young woman
pumping her old veins
with a lie
underneath a bridge
near train tracks

Or why each dancing molecule
is hobbled at the hips
of sun kissed women
shepherded into cathedrals
of stone and glass
made to sit through

classes in compliance

The whys fill up my focus
just like the
the statements dressed up as
questions
that buzz around their projections—
the ones who have no mirror at all—
their thought experiments
always dissonance
pretending to be
something else

I look straight through
what I see
feel the ripples in the self
I can't forget
but can't fully name
a witness and
humble translator
of stolen voices
echoes leaping from the
Atlantic
whispers buried
in every someplace
named after
every somebody
turned speculator of

this body

My mouth
must remain a drum
pounding memory
into the senses
of all who fall
into this puppet show
and believe they pull
their own strings
entangle their knowing
with the acquisition of
things
sleep walk into
high rise coffins
for a husk of a life

We must become the knife
that slices
the gormandizer open
from the inside
recalls the language
of light
whispered into our bones
by the everything
that breathes through us
and never again
forget what we

walk through dreams
trying so desperately
to remember

Zuihitsu I: Survey

survey:
a gathering of a sample of data or opinions
considered to be representative of a whole.
they look skyward, past me
through me,
not to God,
but to see my house
religious people
dressed like death
living in layers that never mesh
with others
the other
the crusted bottom
left in the pan
after cake is flipped onto crystal
for those with confident laughter
and sunglass eyes
we be caramelized
jazz riffed
stew peas and
ripe mango'd
we all good
like dandy lions
bitter and healing
the pansies on the porch

return each year
in spite of the terminator seeds they
sell at Home Depot
there is a chain around my flower pot
croton pulled right out of the dirt
damned ghetto people dem
a layered cake is separated with cream
you can't get your mortgage reduced
this service is for high net worth clients only
I paid for this brick with my sweat
ring my bell, if you think you bad
survey:
chiefly British/to inspect and determine the
structural condition of (a building).
my back broke down in 2008
the way my heart is breaking now
depressed people like a tear gas around me
a true community doesn't use guns to remind its
members to be cohesive
where are we?
when are we?
wherever you go
there you are
there I am
we am
I be we
I is you
get over it

who's your owner?
he peeks into my living room
Weeksville was free before the Civil War
stories are in the floor boards
tell the truth for once
this is a three-story house
who's YOUR owner?
survey:
a gathering of a sample of data or opinions
considered to be representative of a whole.
home is a notion
a dandy lion flower in the breeze
research my frustration
write it in your book
measure it
put it inna yu dictionary
smoke it in yu spliff
I'm traveling
even when I'm standing still
do not
follow
me

Zuihitsu 2: Dying to Live

I'm buying lunch for the kids
they will be better than me
they are limber and brown
they used to call me white girl
I played alone
I'm glad the children are brown—definitely on
one side or the other
It's easier that way
they didn't call me black girl but pretended
I wasn't there
I played alone
my children will be better than me
freer than me
happier than me
I'm buying them lunch
they have more opportunities here
high fructose corn syrup
maltodextrin
the nun called the little brown boy a "mascot"
we won't be going to that school
the teacher says that I probably don't have very
high standards
we won't be staying at that school
she says the teacher told "that man" about my
lazy five year-old son

my husband?
"that man; i don't know who he was."
my husband?
we will be leaving that school
I will teach you everything
milk is on sale
read the food label
soy lechtin
I will feed them things I didn't have
nitrates
omega 3 bread
I'm dying to give them what I didn't have
I'm tired
always tired
high fructose corn syrup
sugar
red no. 5
I'm dying to give them a better life
I'm dying
he's dying
prostate cancer
bladder cancer
we are dying
every moment is a question
silence
the food aisle is always cold
can you die from missing what you don't know?
I don't know my great great gran's name

Mumsie, they did call her
Isabella on paper
queen isabella was a devil
Mumsie mother was on pickney row
the grocery aisle is cold
pickney row
fifty types of sugar, all dressed up
pickney row
a pickney feeds the slaves on the row a bowl of
white mush
cornmeal is just sugar
sugarcane is just sugar
Mumsie say, "wey eva it maaga, it bruk."
my back is hurting again
my daughter sucks her thumb
braces are expensive
I'm tired
I have to have a drink to get through this week
Maya Isabella
Marcus Cornell
they will be better than me

Times Have Been Changed

There is no space
here
to fit your story
like cup to saucer
brick to mortar
New Negro novelty
Afro-American cool

The way has been sealed
times have been changed
for popular consumption
for herding
cajoling
extolling
you masses
made to march through the dark
as you yell from your center
awaiting some echo to bounce back
through madness
like jazz horns
that cradle you
locate you
help you name this feeling
that forms your being

But they tell you
you are too loud
you are
too
much

So you carry everything
in your gaze
that same look
donned by every one of your
mothers
and you tuck it away
until your back
hurts
until this call is an attempt to collect a debt
until the teacher writes "Ritalin" on a piece of
paper
until your breast will have to go
if you want to stay

Yes,

you will stay
you belong
you are sure
like the soil
holding up redwoods
you are essential

you are sure

There is the faintest memory of
star shine and your true reflection
more massive than vocabulary
more dimensional than thought
the ever-laughing black night of your soul
the breath that breathes you
put you here

So clear your throats,
you speakers
you wild women
you oracles
you daughters of Isis
summoned from the black holes
of mother's eyes

Draw your
cutlass and your daggars
clear the space
lance the boils
exhale for the people

For My People

Remember us
that we are dreaming

Sing us now
awake

The Great River

I jumped into the great river
once again,
pulled by love,
through the prism of the womb
and let my furnace
forge this sand house
into a mirror
for this time,
for you,
reflecting what we are
and what we were made to be.

You and me,
we wade
through this stream of consciousness
in search of the sense
in the senseless,
the suffering
caused by those shadow men
who live in their own midnight
and hide in plain sight,
their bellies bursting
with the blood of the
innocent,
their spirits still starving

for understanding
that we don't dwell here,
that we are all the
same drops of light
traveling through the void,
warming each
corner of creation
by being
and believing
that we each
hold a cleansing
super nova,
in the honesty of our eyes,
and that we too
belong in this world,
listened to its first songs,
made music from the humblest of things
and understood that people are not
commodities
but sparks of the divine
set in motion
in a perfect dance,
each day honoring that Great Force
by simply breathing
and loving
and LOVING.

And this inelegant system

that slowly eats itself
can never
stop your breath
because you ARE,
just like Isis is
as Shango is
as Jesus is.
That spirit still lives,
and even the tiniest of lies
can never weave itself into the fabric of life
because life is truth
and light
and the beauty of every living thing
that has ever moved under this sun.

We are not done
because today,
I am We
in this space,
and I want you to see your face
in the mirror of my soul
and wrap these words
around you
like a warm cape
as you blaze through this journey,
living fully in the mystery
of each breath
and knowing that

you reflect the
fullest love
your heart can hold.

Never dwell in those shadows—
be love,
be bold.

We Tumble

We tumble
make thunder
pull down deluges
of discordant dialogue
you and me
oil and water
brick and mortar
who summoned forth
two angels
with our love
but still can't bridge
the gulf
of our resignation
to this banality
that drowns me
in its sameness
and chains me
with its necessity

We must go
inside our selves
you and me
to merge with that
pure essence
original tempest

still locked in a passionate dance
spinning new colors
eternal lovers
caged in the great unconscious
tip toeing to the front of our minds
in the twilight of slumber

I will wait with you
I will wake with you
until the clouds fade away
and you remember
my true name

Witness

Like the memory
deepest hidden,
it drives you

The *you*
you can't put down
make sleep
smother under
logic

The pilot
light inside
burning away
the shapes and masks
that sell you this story—
a spinning web of deja vus
and absurdities

It presses you to
                        Witness
funnel every whirlwind
through your mind's eye
until
from your heart
is wrung

a battle song

But then you see their
hungry mouths
reflections of your mouth
and you bend lower
to hear their
tugging questions
which are also your
questions
even now

So you cradle them
in your mother's laugh
and pretend to know
the whys
and whens
and hows
sending hem satiated
and giggling into another
concrete yard
hoping for a lifetime
before their
joy swings to recognition
of these boxes
that we twirl in
day by day

You stop only to fuel
this vehicle
and not much else
not hearing these words
that jump up
and float uncomfortably
into your staff meeting
you blame the missed coffee
the crowded train
they squint and smirk for manners
sharpen knives under the table

You push down
those ideas that
kick open your
dreams at night
and ripple through
your day
making you
spill the milk
step over the pampers
say to him, "I'm too tired"

You would never give back
your little stars
because "mommy"
is the sweetest serenade
ever sung by God

and so now
they need you
and so always
you give you

But the thoughts still form
and sit on the
shelves of your consciousness
swinging their feet
and cursing at you
until you remember something
of what you are
outside of what you can imagine

The walls of time close in
but you choose to first
season the fish
scrub the toilets
then restrain yourself behind
"Just a second,"
until it becomes a mantra
for running in place
a blueprint you're
determined that your little stars
will never use

Your map
a jagged legacy

sewn together
on a 1970's flight
from palm trees
and anthurium lilies
toward possibilities
followed by latch keys
cold cereal
and warnings
about the body you inhabit
where it can not go
what it should not hope for

But here you are anyway
you checked all the right boxes
and didn't implode
so now you provide
so that they can paint
and play the steel drums
"A truly modern instrument,"
you boast
between mountains of laundry
and multiplying toys

You want someone to pinch you
and then scold yourself
for being ungrateful

So you just

light a candle
write these words
a facsimile
composed in the dark
a rest stop
in the direction of home
where love need not be rationed
where new stories emanate
and create waves
that shift minds into motion
bring life back to
bodies just breathing
see where it hurts
and understand
why that's okay
pull down the sky
and create castles
in the rubble
and just BE
in the only way that
truly matters.

Mama Adisa

I asked Mamma Adisa,
"Is wha' really ah gwaan?"
one night,
when the calluses
of the grind
began burning my temples
and the stench of the streets
and this concrete
hung on me
like another overcoat

and she smiled at me
from that secret room
in the seat of my mind
luminescence in this cave
called society
a memory tucked between
the coils of my hair

and I get to understand
wha' really ah gwaan

inside the space
inside of me
where worlds collide

and vibrate shapes
into the mist
amid the clamor
of disjointed notes
flying freely
from the minds of the
unwieldy
locking themselves into
patterns that flatten
my dream
and the dreamer
who is only the dream
anyway

and she told me to
sing a song of existence
like
wiiri-o, o wiiri-o   *sankoma-aye...*
and watch it twirl through
the clouds
catching hanging notes
and hollow ideas

and to walk my beauty
across the earth
bring the dead to life
through the harmony
that is me

as we settle into this new
now
where Mama Adisa lives
resplendent in gold
a shining temple
of days gone
and days to come

so, the songs must be
written
and sung
in the electricity of
love
that walks through the roads
of your mind
so that there can be
harmony
harmony
not money
not envy
not hypocrisy
just beauty
forming a new
reality
through me
once frightened to be
a seer
and now knowing

I could be nothing else
'cause Mama Adisa
was that same self

again, I am here to
make music
for you
spirit rearranged
and played in
tune
to that one
love song
and before long
we will all
sing ourselves back into
that rainbow
that we used
to know

So, ah jus so it go

For Grandma Joyce (children's poems)

I.

chocolate tea
and hard dough bread
white rum cloth
ties my sick head
naseberry mornings
syrupy sweet
wet red earth
surrounds my feet
shame-a-maka
over granite grave
soursop I planted
still grows in the shade
behind grandma's house
there are
memories in the cracks
oh how I would love
to have her back

II.

Kumina drums
and mannish water
bible songs

through tears
and laughter
dancing mammas
dressed in white
family gathers
for nine night

Percival
will bring the rum
Jack in foreign
couldn't come
Auntie Mavis
squeezes and hugs
I wish I were
a ladybug

I'd fly to mama
across the sea
that's where Sam Sharpe
and Nanny be
she'd give me milk
and grater cake
and two more plantains
on my plate

But this party
isn't so bad
because everyone remembers

how she made them glad

III.

Pick up your toys
Brush your teeth

Study your books
Don't talk while you eat

You say you are tired?
Eh eh! What do you know?

Your great great granny
Was on pickney row

Cutting cane and taking licks
So you could learn arithmetic

Don't turn up your nose at poor Miss Claudine
Is only sin soap and water can't clean

And howdy 'n tenky nuh bruk no square
Try your best and I'll make sure you get there

Now

I'm going to tell
a new story
of have-gots
straight backs
electric loving
us, our-very-selves
no more plastic
3 a.m. rub-a-dub
heads thrown back
cause, ain't it too funny?
and don't worry cause
I. got. this.

I spin this tale
with each stride
to earth rhythm
soul prism
and paint it on the future
let it simmer like
oxtail on a wood stove
spill over itself
like a night blooming
jasmine
in every south
everywhere

you ever been

I will see you there
my friends
and you will
know me
by my smile

Ascension

One day
I will swell
with so much joy
that you won't see me
no more

And my laughter
will be a cool
breeze
on the back of
your bowed head
my dance
a thump in the
hallway
trapped in your
dry gaze
my song
a chuckle in your left ear
before day light
and the flood
of insignificant babble

One day
I will swell
with so much joy

that you won't see me
no more

Tidal Wave

Each restless body
treading this lake of time
roaming this amnesia
looking to own
the place
where clay was
spoken into arms
and legs
and these encrusted hearts
creates a tidal wave
of noise and neon
smoke and sewage
violation and rationalization
that spins us 'round
a creaking wheel
perpetual and
tiny as a peephole

It
must
stop

Do not
keep trickling into
the box

of breath and motion
just to
desire
and acquire
and then
leave the same
way that you came
every time

Open the door
call her name
she who laughs tides into motion
blinks mountains skyward
to touch billowy skirts
blows kisses into
babies' giggles
and makes senses savor
every last herb in the pot

She is the voice waking
in your dreams
promising you
that the face in mirror
is not real
that you are not really here
that you can come home
anytime
if you want

if you're ready
to hold on to each other
each and every one
and swim to the very bottom
deep into the dark
let every accessory
float away
and remember that only you
can know
your true name

About the Author

Keisha-Gaye Anderson is a Jamaican born writer whose works have been published in Renaissance Noire, The Killens Review of Arts and Letters, Small Axe Salon, Streetnotes: Cross Cultural Poetics, African Voices Magazine, Mosaic Literary Magazine, Captured by the City: Perspectives on Urban Culture, Anthology of the Americas Poetry Festival of New York, Afrobeat Journal, Caribbean in Transit Arts Journal, Poetry in Performance, The Mom Egg, Women Writers in Bloom Poetry Salon blog, Bet on Black: African American Women Celebrate Fatherhood in the Age of Barak Obama, Poems on the Road to Peace: A Collective Tribute to Dr. King, and Sometimes Rhythm, Sometimes Blues: Young African Americans on Love, Relationships, Sex and the Search for Mr. Right.

Keisha was a featured reader and participant in the Callaloo Creative Writing workshop for fiction, named a fellow by the North Country Institute for Writers of Color, and short listed for the Small Axe literary competition.

She is also a founding poet with Poets for Ayiti. Proceeds from their 2010 chapbook, For the Crowns of Your Heads, helped to rebuild Bibliothèque du Soleil, a library razed during the earthquake in Haiti.

Keisha holds an M.F.A. in Fiction from The City College, CUNY. She lives in Brooklyn, NY with her husband and two children.

Learn more about Keisha at www.keishagaye.com.

17585815R00067

Made in the USA
Middletown, DE
31 January 2015